THEOR
FUN
FACTORY
3

Katie Elliott

BOOSEY & HAWKES

Welcome to the Theory Fun Factory! In this book you'll find ...

... lots of information about how to read and write music.

... noticeboards which will tell you all you need to know.

... puzzles, puzzles, puzzles!

... characters who'll help you out.

... mystery pages, with all kinds of musical problems to solve.

... a birthday party.

... handy gardening tips.

... the great painter, Vincent van Dogh.

... and a lot more!

CONTENTS

Cover design and layout by Sue Clarke

These words all tell you about the tempo of a piece of music:

andantino	slightly faster than *andante*
larghetto	rather slow (but not as slow as *largo*)
largo	slow, stately
presto	fast (faster than *allegro*)

Here are some other Italian words which you might find useful:

assai	very
con/col	with
ma	but
meno	less
moto/mosso	movement
non troppo	not too much

allegro assai	very quick
allegro ma non troppo	quick, but not too quick
con moto	with movement
meno mosso	less movement, slower

❶ This is a back-to-front crossword. You don't need any questions to solve it because you already have all the answers - but it's up to you to work out where they go!

2 letters: *ma*

3 letters: *con, too*

4 letters: *less, meno, moto, poco, slow, with*

5 letters: *largo, lento, mosso, quick, speed, tempo*

6 letters: *adagio, presto, troppo*

7 letters: *allegro, andante, stately*

8 letters: *moderato, movement*

9 letters: *andantino, larghetto, metronome*

10 letters: *allegretto*

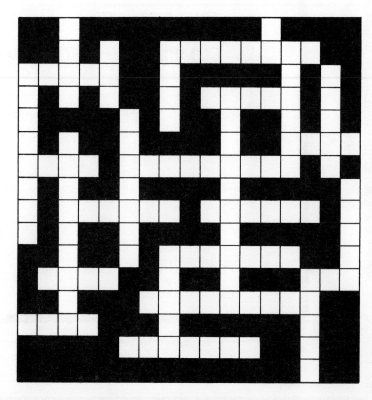

❷ These musical terms all have some letters missing. If you work out what they are and write them in order in the spaces below, you'll find the name of a famous inventor.

LETTERS M_SSI_G!

1. Ma _ _ r scale
2. _ _ lf note
3. A _ danti_o
4. _eno mosso

5. _ll_gro
6. _ento
7. Me_zo
8. Int_rva_

The mystery person is _ _ _ _ _ _ _ _ _ _ _ _ _ _

He is famous for ....

ONCOMING RIDDLE!

❸ Can you work out the hidden word in this riddle?

My first is not found in <u>performs</u> but in <u>plays</u>,
My second's in <u>tune</u>, but it isn't in <u>phrase</u>,
My third is in <u>dots</u> but it's not in <u>staccato</u>,
My fourth's in <u>adagio</u> and <u>moderato</u>,
My fifth's not in <u>triad</u> although it's in <u>tonic</u>,
My sixth may be <u>fast</u>, but it's not <u>supersonic</u>,
My seventh's in <u>interval</u> and in <u>degree</u>,
My whole is a <u>tempo</u> - but what could it be?

The hidden tempo is ....

2 LEDGER LINES

- When notes are too high or too low to fit on the stave, extra lines called **ledger lines** are used. You can work out the name of a note written on ledger lines by counting the lines and spaces.
- Ledger lines never join up, there is always a gap between them so that it is clear which lines make up the actual stave.
- Any note can be written on ledger lines, although the more lines that are used, the harder the music is to read.

4 Copy these notes:

5 I can only read notes in the treble clef. Can you write out these bars so that they are at exactly the same pitch, but are written using the treble clef instead of the bass? Someone has put in the starting note to help you!

 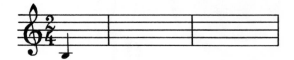

6 Could you rewrite my music too, using the bass clef instead of the treble? Be careful not to change the pitch of the notes, though!

 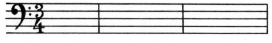

7 If you shade all of the shapes which contain a dot, you'll discover a hidden picture. What is it, and which of the hedgehogs (top or bottom) would prefer to use it?

The picture is a ....
It would be used by the ....
hedgehog.

8 Slug is supposed to be looking after these plants for a friend. Unfortunately, he doesn't know what to feed them and some of them are starting to look a bit ill. Can you help him to work out which type of food is suitable for which plant by matching the pictures on the flower pots to the letter names on the containers of food? Once you've done that, label each pot clearly so that Slug doesn't get them muddled up again!

THE MAJOR SCALES OF A, B♭ AND E♭

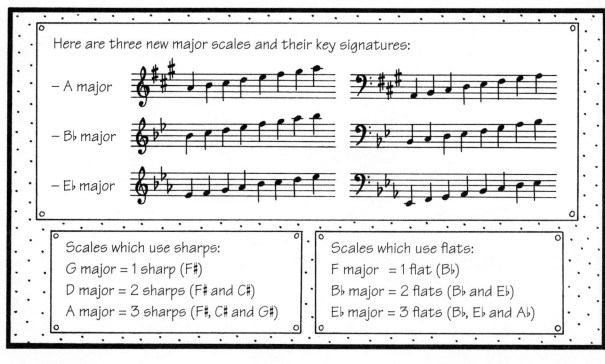

Here are three new major scales and their key signatures:

– A major

– B♭ major

– E♭ major

Scales which use sharps:
G major = 1 sharp (F♯)
D major = 2 sharps (F♯ and C♯)
A major = 3 sharps (F♯, C♯ and G♯)

Scales which use flats:
F major = 1 flat (B♭)
B♭ major = 2 flats (B♭ and E♭)
E♭ major = 3 flats (B♭, E♭ and A♭)

❾ Can you work out, either from the key signature or the accidentals used, which major key each of these bars is in?

10 On each stave write the key signature and the tonic triad of the major key named.

Eb major   A major   Bb major

11 Each chick is humming a scale, not using notes but numbers instead! To work out which they're thinking about, all you need to do is turn all the numbers into notes using this codebox. Then write them out in order and describe the scales you end up with: for example, the descending scale of D major.
(Ascending = going up, descending = going down.)

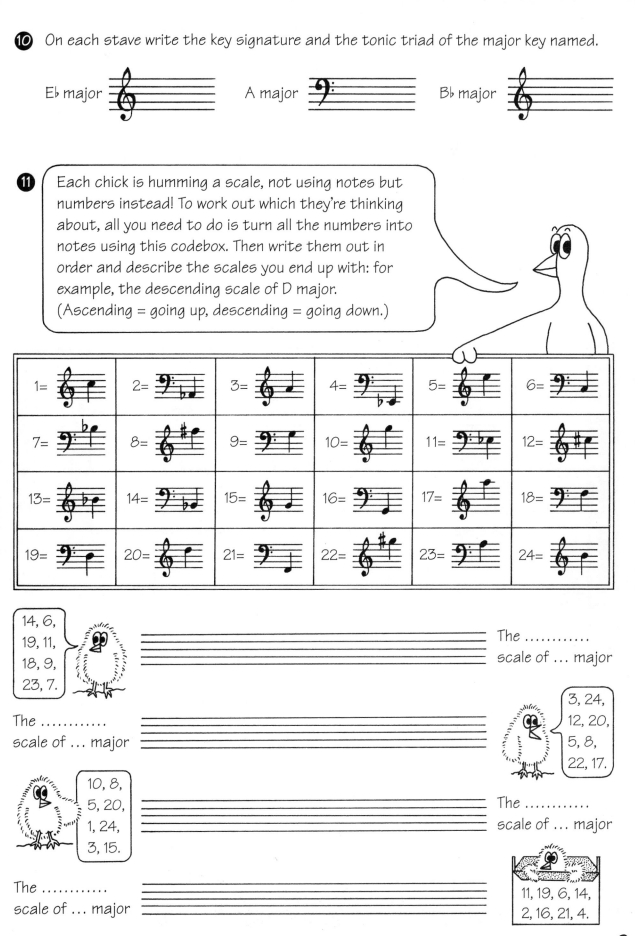

14, 6, 19, 11, 18, 9, 23, 7.

The ....
scale of ... major

The ....
scale of ... major

3, 24, 12, 20, 5, 8, 22, 17.

The ....
scale of ... major

10, 8, 5, 20, 1, 24, 3, 15.

The ....
scale of ... major

The ....
scale of ... major

11, 19, 6, 14, 2, 16, 21, 4.

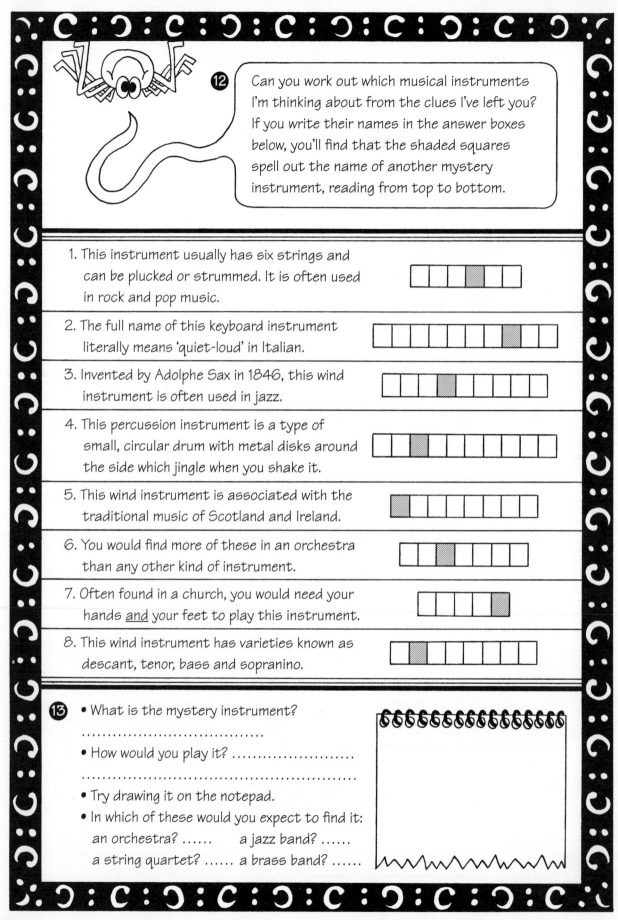

12 Can you work out which musical instruments I'm thinking about from the clues I've left you? If you write their names in the answer boxes below, you'll find that the shaded squares spell out the name of another mystery instrument, reading from top to bottom.

1. This instrument usually has six strings and can be plucked or strummed. It is often used in rock and pop music.

2. The full name of this keyboard instrument literally means 'quiet-loud' in Italian.

3. Invented by Adolphe Sax in 1846, this wind instrument is often used in jazz.

4. This percussion instrument is a type of small, circular drum with metal disks around the side which jingle when you shake it.

5. This wind instrument is associated with the traditional music of Scotland and Ireland.

6. You would find more of these in an orchestra than any other kind of instrument.

7. Often found in a church, you would need your hands <u>and</u> your feet to play this instrument.

8. This wind instrument has varieties known as descant, tenor, bass and sopranino.

13
- What is the mystery instrument?
  ....
- How would you play it? ....
  ....
- Try drawing it on the notepad.
- In which of these would you expect to find it:
  an orchestra? ......   a jazz band? ......
  a string quartet? ...... a brass band? ......

4 INTRODUCING $\frac{2}{2}$ $\frac{3}{2}$ AND $\frac{4}{2}$

– Here are some new time signatures:
$\frac{2}{2}$ = 2 minim (half note) beats in a bar
$\frac{3}{2}$ = 3 minim beats in a bar
$\frac{4}{2}$ = 4 minim beats in a bar
The number 2 at the bottom of each tells you that the type of beat being used is a minim (or half note).

– $\frac{2}{2}$ can also be written like this: ¢.

Hints on grouping notes in $\frac{2}{2}$, $\frac{3}{2}$ and $\frac{4}{2}$:

1. Up to four quavers or semiquavers can be beamed together. However, they can only be joined to others within the <u>same</u> minim beat:

2. Avoid using ties if possible - it's better to use one semibreve than two tied minims.

If music has two beats to a bar ($\frac{2}{2}$ or $\frac{2}{4}$) it is called **duple** time.
If it has three beats to a bar ($\frac{3}{2}$ or $\frac{3}{4}$) it is called **triple** time.
If it has four beats to a bar ($\frac{4}{2}$ or $\frac{4}{4}$) it is called **quadruple** time.

14 Each of these pieces has something missing - it might be a time signature, some bar-lines or even a rest. Can you work out what you need to add to complete them?

15 This piece of music looks wrong because the notes aren't grouped correctly. Try writing it out again, making sure that all the mistakes are put right.

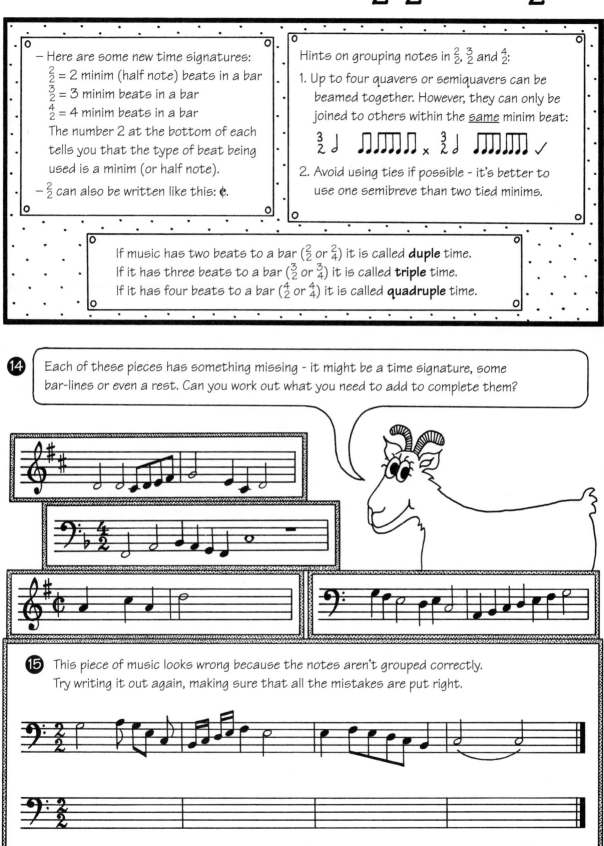

11

5 MOODS IN MUSIC

Here are some Italian words which describe the mood or style of a piece of music:

dolce	sweet, soft
espressivo (*espress.*) }	expressive
giocoso	playful, merry
grave	very slow, solemn
grazioso	graceful
maestoso	majestic
vivace/vivo	lively, quick

These words can be used in longer sentences to explain exactly how you want a piece to be played:

al/alla	in the style of (*alla marcia* = in the style of a march)
e/ed	and
molto	very, much
più	more
senza	without
simile (*sim.*)	in the same way

16 I've come up with a very tricky question for you, but you'll have to solve this wordsearch to find out what it is. Just cross off all the words, collect the unused letters by reading from left to right, line by line and then write them in the spaces below.

__ ___ ____ ___ ____ _____

_____ ___ _____ __ _____?

....

D	E	V	I	S	S	E	R	P	X	E	O
Y	L	M	A	E	S	T	O	S	O	L	O
U	U	E	K	S	N	I	O	O	V	I	V
W	F	C	W	P	H	Y	N	T	M	B	A
M	E	A	G	R	A	V	E	G	D	A	N
A	C	V	H	E	Y	E	E	O	I	T	M
J	A	I	C	S	W	U	L	R	S	N	I
E	R	V	U	S	C	C	U	I	Y	A	G
S	G	G	M	I	E	A	F	L	M	C	W
T	S	L	I	V	E	L	Y	T	S	I	O
I	A	O	S	O	I	Z	A	R	G	R	S
C	D	L	F	S	C	A	L	R	R	E	W
R	M	O	L	T	O	O	P	I	T	E	T
S	E	N	Z	A	E	N	S	I	N	I	M
T	A	L	I	N	M	E	L	O	S	A	N

Alla - Cantabile - Dolce - Espressivo - Expressive - Giocoso - Graceful - Grave - Grazioso - Lively - Maestoso - Majestic - Merry - Molto - Much - Playful - Senza - Simile - Singing - Soft - Solemn - Style - Sweet - Very - Vivace - Vivo

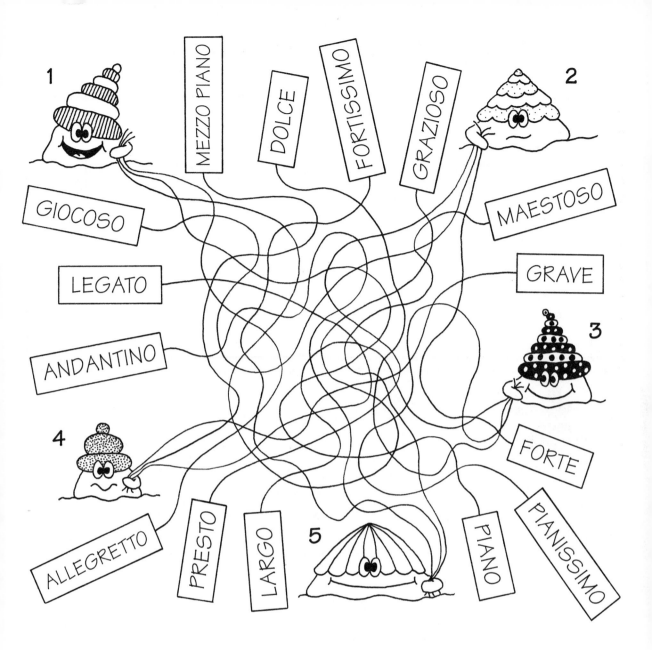

17 These molluscs have each been given three instructions about how to sing their solos in tonight's concert. They've got a bit tangled up in their excitement though, and now they can't work out which words apply to each of them. Can you match up each mollusc to three words and then translate them, just in case they still don't understand? For example, if Mollusc 1 is holding 'mezzo piano', tell him to sing 'quite quietly'.

Mollusc 1 should sing (a) .... (b) .... (c) ....

Mollusc 2 should sing (a) .... (b) .... (c) ....

Mollusc 3 should sing (a) .... (b) .... (c) ....

Mollusc 4 should sing (a) .... (b) .... (c) ....

Mollusc 5 should sing (a) .... (b) .... (c) ....

6 HARMONIC MINOR SCALES

In this chapter you are going to learn how to form a new type of scale called
a **minor** scale. There are two different sorts of minor scale: the **harmonic**
and the **melodic**. We're going to start by looking at the harmonic.

Just like major scales, minor scales all have their own key signature. Here are some
hints to help you work out which key signature goes with each one:
1. Find the note three semitones above the one you want your minor scale to start on.
   (For example, in A minor the note three semitones above A is C.)
2. Then think of the major scale which begins on this note. This scale - known as the
   relative major - has exactly the same key signature as the minor scale you are about
   to write. (C major and A minor both have key signatures of no sharps or flats.)

18 Can you work out the key signatures of the minor scales of E and D, and
then write them on the staves below?

E minor

D minor

Here are three simple steps to follow when you want to form any harmonic minor scale.
1. Write one note on every line and space between your starting and finishing notes.
2. Work out the key signature by thinking of the relative major, and write it on the stave.
3. Now raise the 7th degree of the scale by a semitone. You can do this by putting an
   accidental in front of it - in some cases this will be sharp sign and in others it will be
   a natural.

Here's an example, showing how you could write out the scale of E harmonic minor:

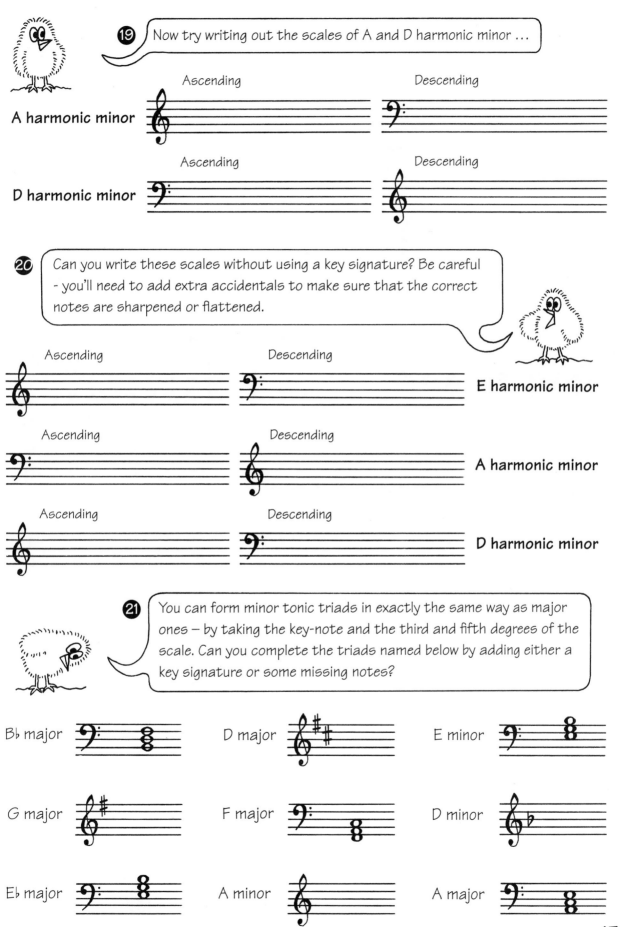

22 Welcome to the studio of the great painter, Vincent van Dogh! Although he's very good at painting, Mr van Dogh is also rather disorganised - he's always so keen to start the next masterpiece that he never gets round to labelling the ones he's already done. Could you finish naming his paintings so everyone knows what they're supposed to be?

The .... degree of the scale of G major

An interval of a ......

The tonic triad of ... major

The key signature of ... major

The scale of ....
....

The scale of ....
....

The key signature of ... major

The tonic triad of ... minor

16

Look closely at this piece of music and then try to answer all the questions about it.

1. What is the key of this piece? ....

2. How many beats are there in each bar? ....

3. What type of beats are they? ....

4. Is the piece in duple, triple or quadruple time? ....

5. What does the word *vivo* mean? ....

6. In which bar can you find all three notes of the tonic triad? ....

7. What is the name of the last note in bar 7? ....

8. Which degree of the scale is this note? ....

9. Which two bars share the same rhythm? ....

7 ANOTHER TIME SIGNATURE: $\frac{3}{8}$

Here is another new time signature: $\frac{3}{8}$. The 3 at the top means that there will be three beats in every bar, and the 8 at the bottom tells you that they will be quaver (eighth note) beats.

When you write out music in $\frac{3}{8}$, you should try to beam notes together where possible. Beam all quavers and semiquavers, whether in groups of just quavers, just semiquavers, or a mixture of the two.

When you beam notes of different pitch, you may find it difficult to decide which direction the stems should go. Always try to beam notes so that the majority of the stems go in the correct direction, even though one or two may become longer or shorter than usual.

24 Rewrite these bars, correcting all the mistakes.

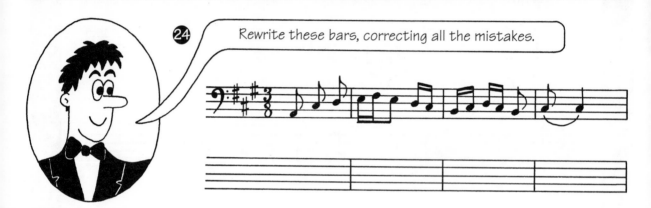

25 This piece is missing some bar-lines. Unfortunately, you won't be able to fill them in until you know what the time signature should be! To work this out, solve the puzzle below and you'll end up with two answers: the top and bottom numbers of the time signature. If the piece starts on the first beat of the bar, where should the missing bar-lines go?

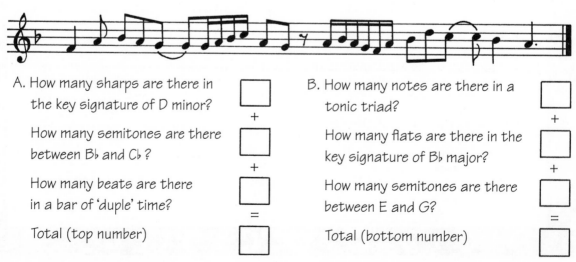

A. How many sharps are there in the key signature of D minor? ☐

+

How many semitones are there between Bb and Cb? ☐

+

How many beats are there in a bar of 'duple' time? ☐

=

Total (top number) ☐

B. How many notes are there in a tonic triad? ☐

+

How many flats are there in the key signature of Bb major? ☐

+

How many semitones are there between E and G? ☐

=

Total (bottom number) ☐

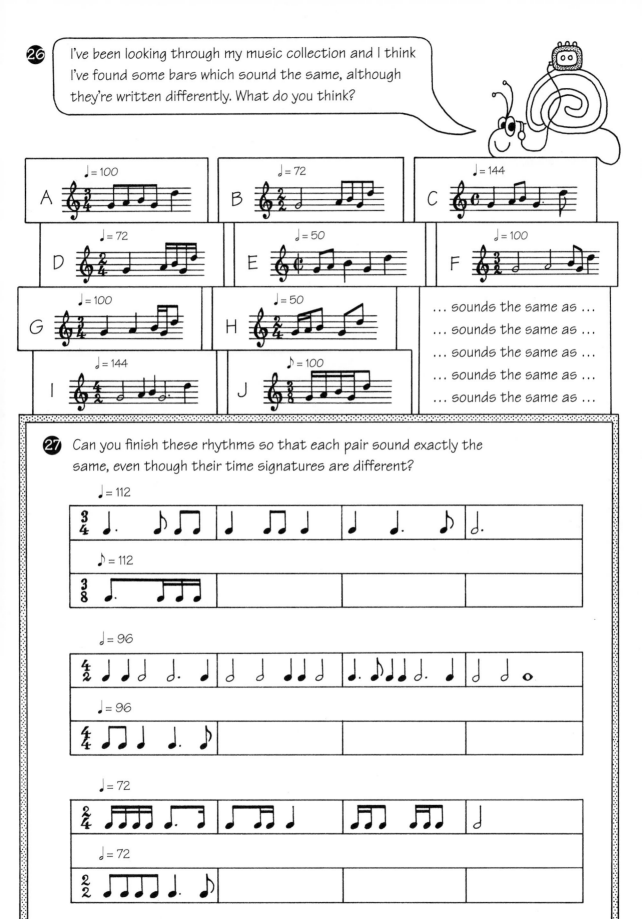

8 NEW WORDS AND SIGNS

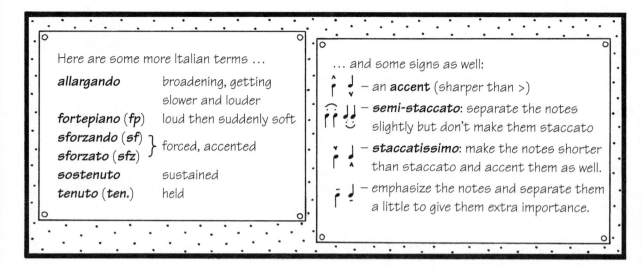

Here are some more Italian terms ...

allargando — broadening, getting slower and louder

fortepiano (fp) — loud then suddenly soft

sforzando (sf)
sforzato (sfz) } forced, accented

sostenuto — sustained

tenuto (ten.) — held

... and some signs as well:

– an **accent** (sharper than >)

– **semi-staccato**: separate the notes slightly but don't make them staccato

– **staccatissimo**: make the notes shorter than staccato and accent them as well.

– emphasize the notes and separate them a little to give them extra importance.

28 Each of these kites contains one item which doesn't fit with the other three. Can you find the odd one out in each case?

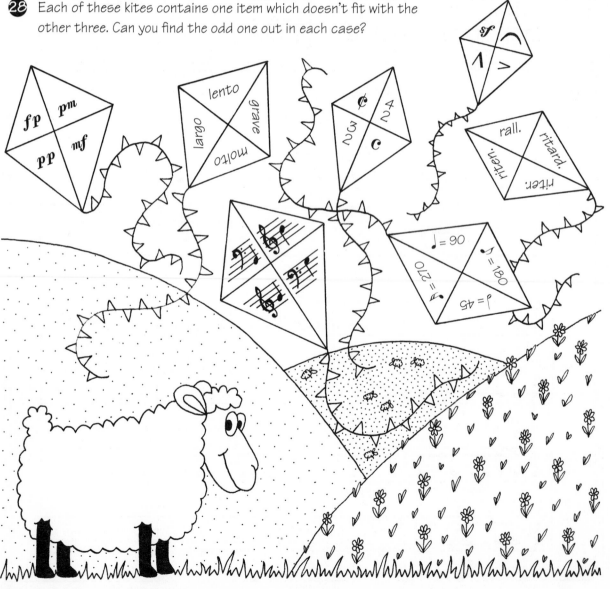

29 I've just finished arranging my collection of musical words to form an alphabet … Can you work out what they all are from the clues I've left you?

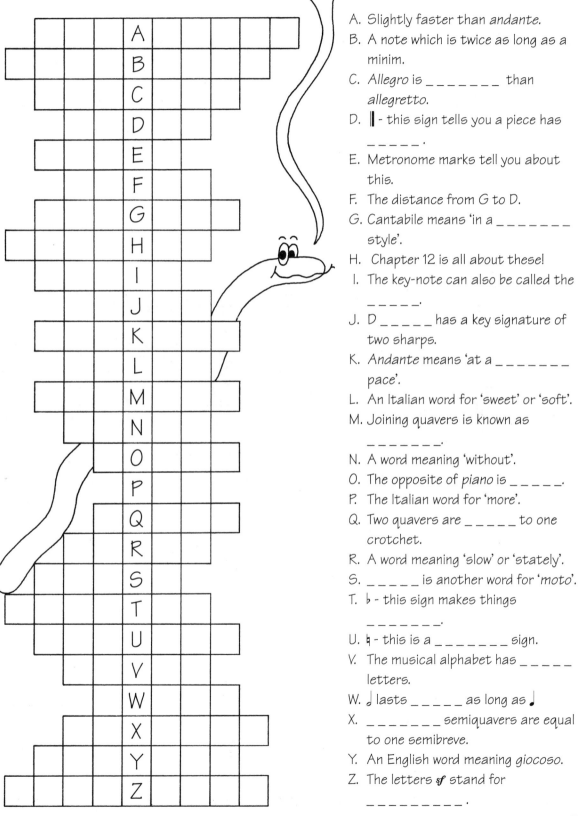

A. Slightly faster than *andante*.

B. A note which is twice as long as a minim.

C. *Allegro* is _ _ _ _ _ _ _ than *allegretto*.

D. ‖ - this sign tells you a piece has _ _ _ _ _ .

E. Metronome marks tell you about this.

F. The distance from G to D.

G. *Cantabile* means 'in a _ _ _ _ _ _ _ style'.

H. Chapter 12 is all about these!

I. The key-note can also be called the _ _ _ _ _ .

J. D _ _ _ _ _ has a key signature of two sharps.

K. *Andante* means 'at a _ _ _ _ _ _ _ pace'.

L. An Italian word for 'sweet' or 'soft'.

M. Joining quavers is known as _ _ _ _ _ _ _ .

N. A word meaning 'without'.

O. The opposite of *piano* is _ _ _ _ _ .

P. The Italian word for 'more'.

Q. Two quavers are _ _ _ _ _ to one crotchet.

R. A word meaning 'slow' or 'stately'.

S. _ _ _ _ _ is another word for '*moto*'.

T. ♭ - this sign makes things _ _ _ _ _ _ _ .

U. ♮ - this is a _ _ _ _ _ _ _ sign.

V. The musical alphabet has _ _ _ _ _ letters.

W. ♩ lasts _ _ _ _ _ as long as ♪

X. _ _ _ _ _ _ _ semiquavers are equal to one semibreve.

Y. An English word meaning *giocoso*.

Z. The letters *sf* stand for _ _ _ _ _ _ _ _ _ .

9 MELODIC MINOR SCALES

Here is another type of minor scale - the **melodic minor**. Unlike the other scales you've learnt so far, the melodic minor uses one set of notes to go up and another to come down. By following the steps below you'll be able to write both the ascending and descending forms of this scale.

1. Write a note on every line and space between your starting and finishing notes.

2. Work out the key signature by thinking of the relative major, and write it in.

3. To write a descending scale: do nothing! - it's already finished.

   To write an ascending scale: raise the 6th and 7th degrees by a semitone.

If you want to write out the scale of E melodic minor you can do it like this:

Be very careful when writing out both forms of the scale on the same stave - make sure that the accidentals you use when <u>ascending</u> don't affect your <u>descending</u> scale as well!

30 Try writing out these melodic minor scales, following the steps above.

22

31 There are lots of keys here, but only one of them will open the biscuit tin. To work out which one, match up each of the pieces below with the key that best describes it. If you pair them all off correctly, the key left over will undo the padlock - and the biscuits will be ours!

E min.

D maj.

F maj.

If a piece is in a minor key you don't say which form of the scale it uses. For example, there isn't a key of A harmonic or A melodic minor - it's just called A minor.

G maj.

D min.

The key to the tin is ....

Bb maj.

A min.

C maj.

32 Write each of the scales described below using the rhythms printed above each stave.

E harmonic minor ascending, <u>with</u> key signature

A major descending, <u>without</u> key signature

D melodic minor ascending, <u>with</u> key signature

Bb major descending, <u>with</u> key signature

A melodic minor ascending, <u>without</u> key signature

D harmonic minor descending, <u>with</u> key signature

24

33 Here are some musical anagrams for you to rearrange. The top words are all pieces of music which you would dance to, and the bottom ones are pieces which you would sing. If you sort them out correctly and write them in the grids, you'll find another piece in each group, by reading the shaded squares from top to bottom.

1. NUTIME

2. OGNAT

3. TWALZ

4. UGGIE

5. HERNIPOP

6. KALOP

7. VAGETTO

The hidden piece is a ....

1. LORCA

2. MHNY

3. ALMAGRID

4. NATTACA

5. SMAS

6. ROATIROO

7. FLOGSNOK

The hidden piece is a ....

10 GROUPING OF RESTS

Here are some guidelines to help you when you write out music of your own. They explain which types of rest to use, and how to group them correctly:

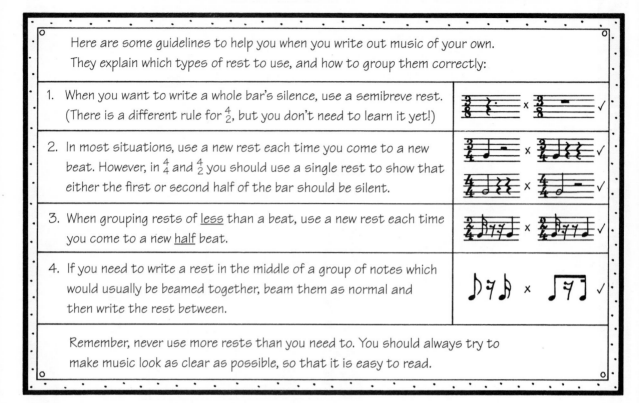

1. When you want to write a whole bar's silence, use a semibreve rest. (There is a different rule for $\frac{4}{2}$, but you don't need to learn it yet!)

2. In most situations, use a new rest each time you come to a new beat. However, in $\frac{4}{4}$ and $\frac{4}{2}$ you should use a single rest to show that either the first or second half of the bar should be silent.

3. When grouping rests of <u>less</u> than a beat, use a new rest each time you come to a new <u>half</u> beat.

4. If you need to write a rest in the middle of a group of notes which would usually be beamed together, beam them as normal and then write the rest between.

Remember, never use more rests than you need to. You should always try to make music look as clear as possible, so that it is easy to read.

34 Can you circle all the mistakes in the piece below, and then rewrite it correctly on the empty stave at the bottom of the page?

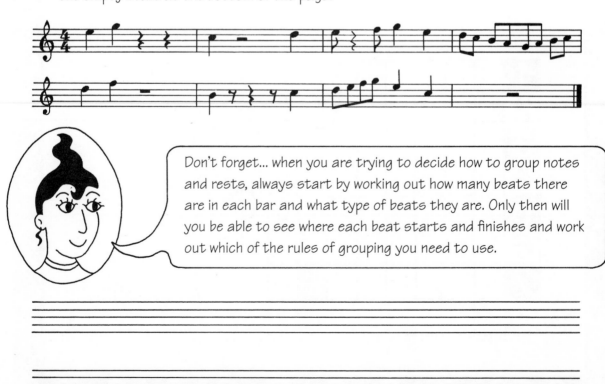

Don't forget... when you are trying to decide how to group notes and rests, always start by working out how many beats there are in each bar and what type of beats they are. Only then will you be able to see where each beat starts and finishes and work out which of the rules of grouping you need to use.

11 TRIPLETS

As you know, any note can be divided to form two new notes of equal length. However, notes can also be split into three parts, known as **triplets**.
Here are some hints on how to form triplets yourself:

1. Work out the note value half as long as your starting note.
2. Write three of this type of note next to one another.
3. Add a small '3' above the middle of the group and unless the notes are already beamed together, write a bracket across the top of them.

Triplets aren't always made up of three equal notes - they can also include rests or notes of different values. As long as you check that the total number of beats is correct, you can form triplets in all sorts of different ways. For example:

(35) Can you find the correct answer to each of the questions below and put a tick in the space next to it?

1. [triplet] lasts as long as: a) ♩   b) 𝅝   c) ♩

2. [triplet] lasts as long as: a) ♪   b) ♩   c) ♪

3. [triplet] lasts as long as: a) ♩   b) ♩   c) ♪

4. [triplet] lasts as long as: a) ♪   b) ♪   c) ♩

(36) Some of the bars in this piece seem to have too many beats. Can you make the notes fit, just by adding triplet signs?

It may not look like it, but this is actually a test ... I just brought in some pot plants to liven it up! Look at the piece below and see how many of my questions you can answer - if you've understood all the work so far you should find them easy!

1. This piece should be played quickly. Which Italian word would you choose to describe it?
....

2. What is the key of the piece? ....

3. What is the relative major of this key?
....

4. In which bar would you find two notes which are an octave apart? ....

5. What is the letter name of the highest note in the piece? ....

6. In which bar would you find the longest note value?
....

7. Which Italian word do the signs in bars 2, 3, 4 and 7 stand for?. ....

8. What does this word mean? ....

9. Write out bars 6 to 8 on the stave below using the time signature provided. Be careful not to change the rhythm.

12 COMPLETING A FOUR-BAR RHYTHM

There are some unfinished four-bar rhythms at the bottom
of the page - can you complete them making sure that:
a) each bar has the correct number of beats
b) they are interesting to listen to?
Below are some hints, to help you work out what to do ...

If you were given the opening rhythm below, you could either:

Method A - choose to copy part of it and combine it with some ideas of your own **or**

Method B - come up with something completely new.

There are hundreds of possibilities whichever method you use, so be adventurous!

38 Complete each of these rhythms twice - once using method A and once using method B.

Remember to avoid finishing on a very short note
- it would make your rhythm sound incomplete.

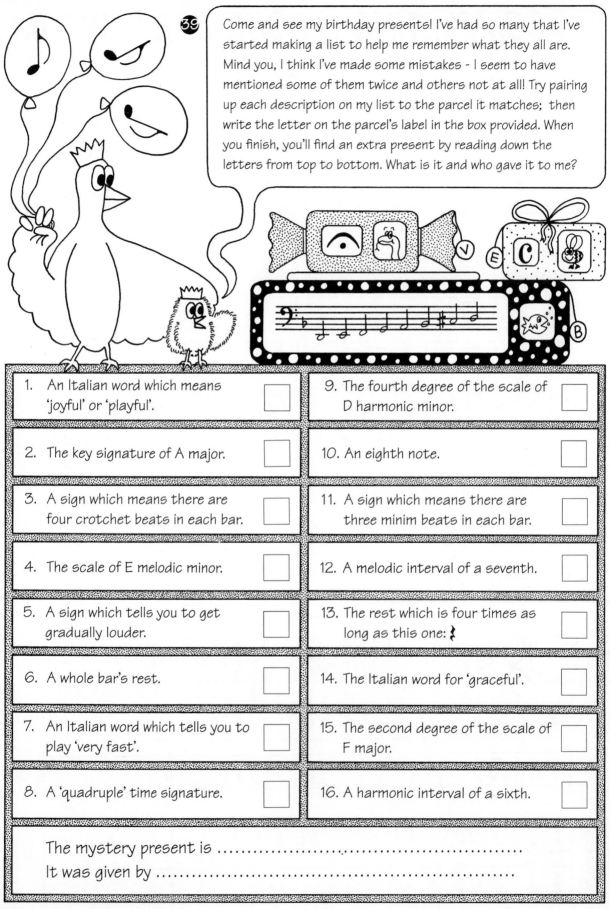

Come and see my birthday presents! I've had so many that I've started making a list to help me remember what they all are. Mind you, I think I've made some mistakes - I seem to have mentioned some of them twice and others not at all! Try pairing up each description on my list to the parcel it matches; then write the letter on the parcel's label in the box provided. When you finish, you'll find an extra present by reading down the letters from top to bottom. What is it and who gave it to me?

1. An Italian word which means 'joyful' or 'playful'.

9. The fourth degree of the scale of D harmonic minor.

2. The key signature of A major.

10. An eighth note.

3. A sign which means there are four crotchet beats in each bar.

11. A sign which means there are three minim beats in each bar.

4. The scale of E melodic minor.

12. A melodic interval of a seventh.

5. A sign which tells you to get gradually louder.

13. The rest which is four times as long as this one: ⸯ

6. A whole bar's rest.

14. The Italian word for 'graceful'.

7. An Italian word which tells you to play 'very fast'.

15. The second degree of the scale of F major.

8. A 'quadruple' time signature.

16. A harmonic interval of a sixth.

The mystery present is ....
It was given by ....

30

ANSWERS

2. Johann Maelzel. He is famous for inventing the metronome.

3. Andante.

7. A bass clef - the bottom hedgehog would use it.

11. B♭ major ascending
    A major ascending
    G major descending
    E♭ major descending.

12. (1) Guitar (2) Pianoforte
    (3) Saxophone
    (4) Tambourine (5) Bagpipes
    (6) Violins (7) Organ
    (8) Recorder.

13. The mystery instrument is a trombone. You would blow it. You might find it in an orchestra, a jazz band or a brass band.

16. The idea of using words to describe the speed or mood of a piece of music began in Italy during the 17th century.

22. (Clockwise) 7th, 5th, D major, E♭ major, A harmonic minor, E minor, A major, F major.

23. (1) E minor (2) 2 (3) Minim
    (4) Duple (5) Lively (6) 6
    (7) D♯ (8) 7th (9) 5 & 6

25. A: 0 + 1 + 2 = 3
    B: 3 + 2 + 3 = 8

26. A = J, B = D, C = I, E = H,
    F = G

28. *pm*, *molto*, **c**, ⌢, riter,
    ♪ = 270, the note B.

29. A. Andantino B. Semibreve
    C. Quicker D. Ended
    E. Speed F. Fifth G. Singing
    H. Rhythms I. Tonic J. Major
    K. Walking L. Dolce
    M. Beaming N. Senza
    O. Forte P. Più Q. Equal
    R. Largo S. Mosso
    T. Flatter U. Natural
    V. Seven W. Twice X. Sixteen
    Y. Playful Z. Sforzando.

31. G major.

33. (1) Minuet (2) Tango
    (3) Waltz (4) Gigue
    (5) Hornpipe (6) Polka
    (7) Gavotte
    The hidden piece = mazurka.
    (1) Carol (2) Hymn
    (3) Madrigal (4) Cantata
    (5) Mass (6) Oratorio
    (7) Folksong
    The hidden piece = chanson.

35. (1) b (2) c (3) a (4) c

37. (1) Allegro (2) D minor
    (3) F major (4) 7 (5) B♭
    (6) 8 (7) Staccato
    (8) Make the notes shorter than usual.

39. The mystery present is the scale of D major. It was given by the dog.

Printed by
Halstan & Co. Ltd., Amersham, Bucks., England